THE
DEMENTIA
Caregiver's
SURVIVAL
GUIDE

Susan Wilson Krechel M.D.

THE DEMENTIA *Caregiver's* SURVIVAL GUIDE

Charleston, SC
www.PalmettoPublishing.com

The Dementia Caregiver's Survival Guide

Copyright © 2023 by Susan Wilson Krechel M.D.

All rights reserved

No portion of this book may be reproduced, stored in a retrieval system, or transmitted in any form by any means—electronic, mechanical, photocopy, recording, or other—except for brief quotations in printed reviews, without prior permission of the author.

First Edition

Paperback ISBN: 979-8-8229-1636-4
eBook ISBN: 979-8-8229-1637-1

Table of Contents

Introduction 1
Chapter 1   How to Avoid Dementia at Any Age 3
Chapter 2   The Most Important Things
             You Need to Know. 10
Chapter 3   Getting the Help You Need. 20
Chapter 4   How to Deal with the Unexpected 29
Chapter 5   Palliative Care and Hospice. 34
Chapter 6   Grief. 36
Chapter 7   News from the Front Lines of
             Research. 39
Chapter 8   Pearls of Wisdom. 44

Introduction

This book is for those who have the privileged and demanding job of caring for a loved one who has dementia.

I have not included the references to specific scientific studies that I have reviewed in order to formulate this guide. These can be found in my previous book, *How to Navigate the Minefield That Is Dementia with Your Loved One*, available on Amazon or on my Facebook page, Navigating Dementia.

My focus is on you, the caregiver. I know from my own experience that the caregiver is often overlooked. The emotional, physical, and financial toll of taking care of a patient with dementia is great.

My goal is to help you find joy in your task. This will help both you and your loved one. I will outline steps you can take to protect your own health and wealth. Finally, I will give you tips on how to deal with some of the inevitable problems that you will encounter. For example, how do you respond the first time your loved one does not know who you are?

I will start with something that may be alarming to you, and that is how you can avoid dementia.

Statistically speaking, you as a caregiver are 1.5 to 2 times more likely to develop dementia than a non-caregiver. As husband, wife, son, or daughter, you have shared a significant part of your lives together. Whatever the cause or causes of dementia may be, you may well share in the environment from which the dementia has sprung.

CHAPTER 1

How to Avoid Dementia at Any Age

1. Make sure your blood pressure is under control.

What does that mean? It means every time you take your blood pressure, it reads 120/80 or less (110/60 or 115/70, for example). I said every time *you* take your blood pressure; you need to own a device to take your blood pressure. These devices are inexpensive and easy to use. Take your blood pressure once or twice a week. If your readings are not 120/80 or less, then call your doctor. He or she may want to begin therapy with a blood pressure medication, increase your dose of blood pressure medication if you are already on a medication, or add another blood pressure medication. I have taken as many as three different blood pressure medications every day to keep my blood pressure under control.

Why is this important, you ask? When blood pressure is not controlled within a narrow range, small blood vessels within the brain can rupture, literally causing small strokes. Typically there are no symptoms, but each time the brain is damaged, it leads to the real possibility of vascular dementia. In fact, nearly all cases of dementia involve some element of vascular dementia.

2. Follow the MIND diet.

The MIND diet combines elements of the Mediterranean diet and the DASH diet. It is a low-salt diet that includes whole grains, fruits, vegetables, beans, nuts, olive oil, moderate amounts of fish, and low to moderate amounts of red wine and greatly limits red meats, dairy products, animal fats, and processed food. Some salt is necessary in our diets, but it should not be used in excess. Nearly all processed foods and restaurant foods are loaded with salt (because it tastes good). In excess, salt raises your blood pressure and makes you retain water.

The typical Western diet, heavy on carbs and fat, is not healthy. Cheeseburgers, fries, red meat, and sugar-laden desserts and beverages need to go. They may be comfort foods, but they are not going to keep you healthy.

My special weakness is french fries. Yes, I indulge once in a while. As a special treat, I will have fries with my veggie burger.

Science is just now beginning to understand why diet is so important. Our intestinal tract is lined with bacteria and other microbes, and we form a symbiotic relationship with these microbes. They produce substances that we need and cannot make ourselves, and we in turn feed them. It is possible to harm the beneficial microbes in our gut with antibiotics and antibacterials. These microbes thrive on the nutrients and fiber found in fruits and vegetables in the Mediterranean diet. They do not do well with the typical Western diet.

Why not just repopulate these microbes with a probiotic pill, you may ask? We are still learning about which microbes and which balance is best for each individual, so for now the best practice is to follow the MIND diet and eat a very large variety of fruits (including several servings of berries a week) and vegetables.

3. Avoid sugar!

Excess sugar consumption leads to type 2 diabetes, obesity, and insulin resistance. Insulin is part of the signaling process in the normal brain. Insulin resistance found in patients with dementia results in the signals from one brain cell to the next proceeding abnormally. Some refer to dementia as type 3 diabetes.

Unfortunately sugar substitutes are not the answer. These have been shown to be harmful to our gut microbes. So curb your sweet tooth. You can do it!

4. Make sure that you get eight hours of sleep every night.

This is critical. The brain cleanses itself only during deep sleep. Specialized cells in the brain literally take out the trash every night. If this cellular trash is allowed to build up, it disrupts the normal brain signaling process.

Our bodies are designed to sleep at night, not during the day. Get your z's!

5. Take the time to exercise every day.

A multitude of studies suggest that those who exercise daily are much more likely to avoid dementia. Yoga, Pilates, tai chi, or simply walking are great ways to accomplish this goal. I make it a point to walk two to four miles every day. Start slow and build your stamina. You will not only help yourself avoid dementia, but you will feel better too. Exercise leads to the release of all sorts of feel-good substances in your body.

6. Get your vaccines.

Viruses especially and other microbes such as bacteria, spirochetes, fungi, and prions all tend to find their way to the brain. Some never leave; for example, the chicken pox virus remains and in later life may cause shingles. Some experimental work suggests that the damage these microbes do may bring on a cascade of brain changes, leading to dementia.

7. Avoid air pollution.

This is easier said than done in our modern society. Almost anywhere you live, there is pollution in one form or another. Mexico City is the most polluted city on the planet, and studies have shown that brain changes associated with dementia are found in children in Mexico City, some as young as six months old. These changes are not seen in children living in rural Mexico. When air quality is poor, wear a mask.

8. Maintain a social life.

This, too, is hard for the caregiver. In my own case, I found most of my friends avoided me and my husband after he developed dementia. I found I had to create a new social life for the two of us. I found that we were both welcomed at church activities and as volunteers for charitable organizations. This gave both of us a social outlet and allowed me to watch over him as well. The brain does not function well in isolation. Get out there and do the things that give you contact with other people.

9. Learn something new.

This is exercising your brain. Sometimes the difference between dementia and no dementia is brain reserve capacity. By learning new things, you are building that reserve capacity. New circuits and pathways are being created in the brain. Learn a new language or take up a musical instrument. Yes, you can do it while still caring for your loved one.

10. Be sure to take care of your vision and hearing.

If you cannot see or hear clearly, it is difficult to socialize and to learn new things.

Everything that I have outlined above is evidence based; that is, scientific studies suggest these actions lead to a decrease in the incidence of dementia. You might ask: Will these actions reverse dementia in my loved one? No, they will not reverse dementia, though it does seem reasonable to expect that these actions could slow the rate of decline in patients with dementia. Studies have not yet been conducted to prove or disprove this theory. However, two can play at all these activities. Take your loved one with you as you make this journey toward a dementia-free tomorrow.

CHAPTER 2

The Most Important Things You Need to Know

A basic understanding of the disease process will help you cope with day-to-day challenges and help both you and your loved one find joy instead of sorrow.

1. Dementia is aging in reverse.

Understanding this will help temper some of the frustration you may feel as you watch the mental decline. To those taking care of parents, the parent-child roles seem reversed. They are. We understand children and instinctively know how to treat them with patience and love. As you watch your loved one progress through dementia, you will be able to identify the unruly risk-taking teenager early in the process. Confrontation is no more appropriate here than in the case of the teenager. *Patience!* All too soon you see the totally dependent child who follows you everywhere and becomes very anxious if you are not in sight.

To keep your loved one entertained, you may need to consult the toy box. The five-hundred-piece puzzle is likely too hard. Get out the ten-piece Spider-Man puzzle. They will love it. Teddy bears and baby dolls can be a great comfort too.

While your loved one has the mental age of a child and you need to provide age-appropriate materials, people with dementia are still adults, and it is important not to treat them like children. Perhaps the most important difference is that someone with dementia cannot learn. Most of our interactions with children are teaching moments. Not so with those who have dementia. Patience and understanding are the keys to quality of life for both of you.

2. Quality of life, not quantity of life, is important.

Our first thought is always to protect our loved one. But doing so may seriously interfere with our loved one's quality of life. Being able to take risks is an important part of life. To some extent it makes us feel more alive. Simple things are now risky for the person with dementia. Taking a walk is risky; he or she may not be able to find their way home. Still, you cannot lock them up. There is no cure for dementia; your loved one will die from the disease. Do everything you can to mitigate the danger without diminishing the quality of life.

Cell phones are actually pretty complicated pieces of equipment, and the person with dementia is soon baffled by the technology. I purchased a flip phone for my husband and put myself and his two daughters on speed dial: one for Susan, two for Claudia, and three for Gloria. That worked well for a while. He was proud and happy to be able to call one of us anytime he wanted.

When that no longer worked, we went to a medical alert device. There are many on the market. Be sure you get one that will meet your needs. Some only work within a few feet of the home. Some advertise that they will work anywhere, but that is anywhere you can get a signal. The other problem with these devices for people with dementia is the fact that they will frequently discard them for no reason. Threshold alarm wristbands can be used so that you are alerted when your loved one is about to leave the house. These devices can be adjusted so that they cannot be removed. You can then go for that walk with them or at least be sure they are properly attired for their adventure.

The ability to accomplish something is also a human need. Let your loved one help you with the housework, the laundry, or whatever else you are doing.

If the task they perform is not up to your standards, thank them and redo the task when they are not looking. Just as volunteer tasks were helpful for me, so were they helpful for my husband. He felt useful and satisfied helping me at a local food bank. In my experience these volunteer organizations welcomed both of us even though his abilities were different from those of others.

I found that this need to accomplish something was so great that my husband would fantasize about accomplishing something even when he was in a veterans' home. I asked him once what he had been doing that day, and he explained that he had gotten all the guys fed that morning at breakfast. Believing that he had accomplished something that day was important to his sense of well-being.

Always treat your loved one as if he or she is behaving normally, even if they are not. Constant reminders that they are no longer normal simply robs them of their dignity.

3. It is important not to point out the reality when your loved one is undergoing a fantasy.

Fantasies and hallucinations are quite common in the later stages of dementia and may occur earlier.

When your loved one is experiencing this, pointing out the reality tends to create anxiety at best and anger at worst. Sometimes hallucinations are anxiety provoking. If they see bugs on the wall or snakes on the floor, make a show of removing the offending object. Fortunately for me and my husband, his hallucinations were always looked upon as interesting and wondrous.

4. There are pharmaceuticals available to treat the behavioral symptoms of dementia, but in my own view, psychotherapy and calming reassurances are enough to treat these symptoms.

Anxiety, depression, and inappropriate behaviors are extremely common in moderate and late-stage dementia. Would you drug your two-year-old who has a tantrum? Not very likely. Physicians frequently ordered mind-altering drugs for my husband. It completely removed him from reality. He simply slept in his chair. When I convinced them to take him off these drugs, he emerged from his semi coma to become a functioning human being once more. Resist the attempts by others to use mind-altering pharmaceuticals to treat your loved one.

5. There will come a time when you must protect others from your loved one with dementia.

You will need to take away the car keys. There will come a time when the rapid information processing needed to safely drive a car is no longer available to your loved one. Don't let this be a prison sentence. Encourage other forms of transportation such as taking the bus, a taxi, or a rideshare; walking; or catching rides with friends or family. I was fortunate; my husband gave up the keys voluntarily. For other people with dementia it is not so easy, but it is critical for their own and others' safety.

6. Mind, body, and spirit are connected; building one will build the others.

As your loved one's mind declines, building up his or her body and spirit will pay dividends for both of you. Exercise is critical. I spent countless hours helping my husband to stay strong and fit. Walking and using the treadmill were very helpful in improving his functional capacity. The stronger he became, the more capable his mind was.

Music is a wonderful way to reach the spirit. Even when the end is near, music improves life.

7. *Withhold* your help whenever possible.

I know that does not sound right, but you will be doing both of you a great service by withholding your help in certain situations. Keep your loved one independently bathing, dressing, and even taking his or her medicine as long as possible. Being able to do these things dramatically lifts their self-esteem. My husband was able to do all these things well into the late stages of moderate dementia. As soon as he entered assisted living and others began helping with these tasks, he lost his ability to care for himself, and the loss of self-esteem was devastating for both of us.

8. You must plan ahead.

It is very likely that your loved one will eventually need more care than you can provide. This may actually happen suddenly, because you will make adjustments until there are no more adjustments to be made. In reality it has not come about suddenly; it just seems that way. If you have not done the hard work of planning ahead, you and your loved one will find yourselves at risk both physically and financially.

Consult an elder care attorney as soon as you receive the dementia diagnosis. You will need to have power of attorney documents drawn up. Unless you have these, your loved one will have a court-appointed guardian to make all necessary decisions, including sale of assets to pay for care. Care can cost upward of $10,000 per month. If your loved one is your spouse, certain assets are protected as long as you are living but will automatically become the property of the state if your loved one needs to go on Medicaid. This enables the state to recoup some or all of the costs it incurred under Medicaid rules. The house will not pass to the children as you may have planned. All this can be avoided with proper planning, and the elder care attorney will be able to help you achieve your goals.

Do not wait until the need arises to look for a skilled nursing home, adult day care, or assisted living facility. They usually have waiting lists that may be months long. Some will be unavailable to you and your loved one. Find the best fit and get on the waiting list. If your name comes up and you are not yet ready, just ask to be placed at the bottom of the list again. I suggest that you get on the waiting list for several facilities.

Do your homework when evaluating these facilities. Many are privately owned and operated, and they are free to pick and choose their clients. They do not serve Medicaid patients. All of them reserve the right to transfer patients to psychiatric hospitals if behavior becomes an issue, and most will not allow the patient to return. Only some assisted living facilities offer rehabilitation services, so if your loved one goes to a hospital and needs rehabilitation afterward (and they almost always do), you will need to find a place for rehabilitation care while still paying for the unoccupied room at the assisted living facility. If your loved one or their spouse was in the military, there may be veterans' benefits available, and a veterans' home may be the perfect option for skilled nursing care. My husband was a resident of several memory care, day care, and assisted living homes. The best one was the Missouri Veterans Home.

9. Nothing you do or do not do will change the course of dementia.

You should never have regrets. Do the best you can. Negative thoughts will come to your mind. They still come to mine. You must banish them. The brain controls everything; it controls breathing and the beating heart. In the end, the brain will shut things down completely. Death is the natural conclusion of dementia.

10. When your loved one's journey with dementia has ended, move on with your life.

Your loved one would want only the best for you. You will never forget them. Honor them by living your life.

CHAPTER 3

Getting the Help You Need

Yes, you will need help—and lots of it. It may or may not take a village to raise a child, but it most certainly takes a village to care for an adult with dementia.

1. Consult an elder care attorney as soon as the diagnosis is confirmed.

At an early stage, your loved one is still mentally competent. You will want them to participate in the estate planning. Their wants and needs can be incorporated into the planning documents. These documents will be critical when your loved one is no longer mentally competent and able to make these decisions on their own. Declaring them incompetent is easy to do; you need one or sometimes two physicians to certify that someone is no longer mentally competent.

Having my husband declared incompetent was a gut-wrenching decision for me. My husband was mentally incompetent long before I asked that he be declared as such. For me, it was a psychological bridge that I did not want to cross. It meant accepting the inevitable and putting the whole load on my shoulders. But eventually, it must be done.

2. It is likely that your support networks will fail you when you need them most.

We all have networks of friends and family. The vast majority of people do not understand dementia. Consequently they fear it and do not want to be reminded that this could one day be their own fate. They will stay away. You will be alone.

Those of us who write books about dementia are connected to you and to each other through AlzAuthors.com. Our collective goal is to educate people and remove the stigma associated with dementia. Each author brings a unique body of knowledge and experience to their writings. *Read*; we want to *help*.

3. At some time in your journey, you may need in-home caregivers to care for your loved one.

You may enlist in-home caregivers to allow you to do other things you need to do that cannot include your loved one. In my case, the first time I needed in-home care was to get some sleep. My dear husband was constantly waking me up at night. I simply was not getting the sleep I needed. My first call was to Visiting Angels on Thanksgiving Day. The franchise owner was at my house that evening to evaluate our needs, and they began providing caregivers to sit with him at night from 10:00 p.m. to 7:00 a.m. In the morning before they left, they would help him shower and get dressed. Within a month he was sleeping through the night, and we did not need them anymore.

BrightStar is another provider agency you can call upon to help you on a regular basis or just through a rough patch. There are many such agencies. Some are nationwide franchises, such as the ones mentioned above, and some are local businesses seeking to fill the needs of our aging population.

You may well be able to find individuals who will do in-home care. Ask around; friends, clergies, or beauticians may know someone who will do this kind of work. Typically they charge by the hour and will do bathing, dressing, and toileting as well as simple meal preparation. As opposed to getting assistance from agencies, the upside to hiring an individual is that the person is the same each time, and this is usually more economical. The downside is that there is no flexibility; if the individual is sick, there is no backup, you will need to perform all the tasks yourself, and twenty-four-hour coverage is not possible.

4. Respite care is another option you should become familiar with.

Respite care is a short-term nursing home placement. If you need a vacation from your caregiver role but are not yet ready to have your loved one enter a skilled nursing facility, many of these facilities will admit your loved one for a two-to-three week stay. Advance planning is required; the demand for these services is higher than the supply.

Beware: if you do this, your task may be harder when your loved one returns. He or she may lose the ability to bathe, dress, or do other skills he or she was able to do previously. I tried this route once with my husband. Everything was all set for him to receive care while I had a surgical procedure. While he initially agreed to this short-term arrangement, he began acting out in ways that were unbearable. I canceled the stay and contacted Visiting Angels once again. They provided twenty-four-hour care for both of us while I was recuperating from surgery.

5. Adult day care is another valuable tool for care.

Many adult day cares provide all the services that one could possibly need. Pickup and delivery from home to the center may be available. A registered nurse is available to give medications and assist with medical emergencies. Breakfast and lunch are provided, and brain-age-appropriate activities are also provided. In moderate-stage dementia, my husband loved it. The socialization was actually very beneficial to him, awakening skills and memories that had been dormant awhile.

A full-service adult day care facility is likely to cost you between $20,000 and $30,000 per year. If this allows you to continue with your job and career, it is well worth it. There are adult day care centers associated with churches and communities. These cost much less but offer limited services and, in many cases, offer only half-day sessions.

6. At some point you will simply not be able to provide the care your loved one needs, even with the outside help described above.

The task is simply too exhausting and too detrimental to your own health. Now, there are several types of facilities and dozens of individual facilities to choose from. For me, the task was nothing short of mind numbing. I looked and looked and studied and studied. No two were alike, and no consistent sets of regulations were to be found, but every one of them had plenty of rules and regulations. If you do not ask the right questions, you will only become aware of these rules when they are applied to your loved one, and you will find them removed from the facility and forbidden to return.

Yes, the reality is harsh. It was only after having all these harsh realities impact my husband and me, and after investigating dozens of facilities, that I learned there are professionals out there who can help you find the right place for your loved one.

A Place for Mom and Caring.com are two of the online agencies that come to mind. I found them helpful. These are nationwide agencies, and the person you talk with may be anywhere, but there are times when talking to someone, anyone who has some idea of what you need, is very comforting. These online services are free of charge; the company is paid only after you have signed a contract with a facility they've recommended.

Since my husband, Ollie, was a veteran, they also gave me information on veterans' aid and even connected me with a VA representative. The online services can give you the names and locations of facilities near you, but they have no firsthand knowledge of these places. If you live close to a state border, you may be given the names of facilities in more than one state. Beware of deciding upon a facility located in a state in which you do not reside. It may be fine for a while, but if you eventually need Medicaid, you will not be eligible for Medicaid assistance in a state you do not live in.

Look for people with a certification from the Society of Certified Senior Advisors (CSA). You will find one or more of these individuals in your area. They work exclusively with facilities in their own areas and are familiar with each one, allowing them to help you find the best fit for you and your loved one. For me, it was comforting to be face-to-face with someone who understood the problem and could help find solutions. They also work free of charge for patients and their families and are paid by the facility you choose.

If you or your loved one has been in the military, don't forget to explore your options for military care. In addition to Veterans Affairs care homes, there are veterans' homes in every state. Many of these state-run homes have been in existence since the Civil War. They are run under the guidelines specified by the US Department of Veterans Affairs but are separate entities.

Each will have its unique features. My husband spent his last days in one of Missouri's veterans' homes. He was very well cared for, and the cost was surprisingly little. Depending on your circumstances, it may even be free.

I strongly advise that you check out available facilities well before you need them and get your loved one on the waiting list for admission. If you are not yet ready when they call, just go to the bottom of the list. If you wait until you need placement, there will be nothing available, with the exception of places you do not want your loved one living in.

When you tour facilities, be sure to ask the hard questions. What happens if, for example, your loved one has behavioral issues? What is the process for dealing with them? You may be surprised to hear that your loved one will be sent to a psychiatric hospital and will not be allowed to return to this facility. Better have a plan B. Another question to ask: What happens if we run out of money? Private facilities will tell you that if the bills are not paid, your loved one will be put on your doorstep. The private facilities do not accept Medicaid patients and will not help you navigate that system. This is one of the many reasons that I suggested consulting an elder care attorney as soon as the dementia diagnosis is made.

Be sure the facility you choose has a dementia-friendly rehabilitation unit associated with it, or you may find that you either give up the room you have been paying for or pay for an empty room while your loved one undergoes post hospitalization rehabilitation services.

CHAPTER 4

How to Deal with the Unexpected

Not Being Recognized

We all believe that our loved one will always remember who we are. We all feel that our own relationship is deeper and more loving than that of others. Unfortunately, your loved one *will* fail to recognize you at various times during the illness. It always comes as a shock, and it is always painful.

The first time my husband did not recognize me, we were leaving a big-box store. I was holding his hand because doing so made it easier for me to keep track of him. He said to me, "My wife would not like this."

"I am your wife," I said. He did not believe me. At first it struck me as funny, and then it hit me: he did not recognize me. By the time we arrived at home, he at least accepted my story.

This was not a major incident, but it could have been. My husband allowed me to guide him to the car and got in. What if he had not? Did I have a plan? No, I did not. I can tell you this from experience: always remain calm. If you become agitated, so will your loved one. Among the last brain functions to leave are the lower centers governing the fight-or-flight reflexes. If these kick in, someone is likely to get hurt. Before things escalate in an uncontrolled environment, be prepared to call 911. If you are in a controlled environment, such as your home, simply leaving the room will often de-escalate the situation.

Sometimes your loved one will simply forget your name. That is when you will hear terms of endearment that you may not have heard in a while. Once, when asked if he knew who I was, Ollie stated, "Yes, that is my second wife." We had been married thirty-six years. That hurt; he remembered his first wife but not my name.

Sometimes they will recognize that you are a significant person in their life, but they do not know what that significance is. In this case they may use polite but not endearing terms. Once, when I was on a visit to the veterans' home where my husband resided, he referred to me as "beautiful woman."

Be prepared for the time when you kiss them goodbye and they react in a shocked, even appalled way. The key here is to be prepared. It will happen.

You will be hurt, but remember: your loved one is not deliberately hurting you. It is simply part of the disease's course.

Falls

Another common problem is falling. If your loved one is not falling, it may mean you or someone else is restricting their movement too much. If you venture to live, you venture to fall. Quality of life is much more important than quantity of life.

Be prepared with a bit of first aid. Seldom do they really hurt themselves. If they do have a significant injury, like a child they will cry out in pain repeatedly. A serious injury that requires a call to 911 is usually pretty obvious.

Getting your loved one up off the ground or floor may be very challenging. While it may take several requests, you can usually find a stranger willing to assist you if you are in a public location. If this is not possible and you are outside and the weather is too hot or too cold, you may need to call 911. Often your loved one can get up by themselves with some encouragement if you give them time. For example, they may use a nearby object to help pull themselves up.

It was my experience that my husband fell frequently in the house. The floors were carpeted and warm, so it was relatively easy to wait until he was able to get himself up. Sometimes I would move a chair to his location and encourage him to pull himself up. Sometimes he simply did not want to try. I would let him lie there until he was ready. If your home is on a slab, this is not an option. Lying on a concrete slab for any length of time may lead to hypothermia. Your only option in this case is to call for assistance: a neighbor, a friend, or a family member, or if no one is readily available, you should call 911.

Toileting

In late-moderate and late-stage dementia, toileting becomes a problem. At home you may need to help your loved one with their underwear. If the lid is kept down on the toilet, it is not unusual for a person with dementia to have bowel movements on top of the lid.

If you are out at a theater or restaurant, you may find that you need to accompany your loved one to the restroom. I saw the inside of many men's restrooms with and without other men present. With the new trend of unisex bathrooms, this will become much less of a problem.

Keep in mind, your loved one is aging in reverse. You are caring for a large child. Knowing this makes the task easier.

Inappropriate Behaviors

You may encounter the removal of clothing in public, kicking, biting, scratching, and similar behaviors. If these occur in public, it is a spectacle. We've all witnessed this behavior in children. Do not be embarrassed. If need be, simply comment that your loved one has dementia and a brain age of two. Dementia is a very common condition, and many people have experienced it with their own families.

Remove your loved one from any public environment as quickly as you can. Distract their attention, but do so very calmly. This is probably the same thing you would do with a toddler. If you are at home, remove yourself from the room. This will quickly defuse any situation.

Sometimes these behaviors are related to some unexpressed need such as hunger, thirst, or uncomfortable sensations your loved one can no longer express. Make an attempt to figure out what is causing the behavior. In my husband's case, the root cause was often a urinary tract infection. This is very common in elderly patients with dementia.

This chapter is intended to help you deal with the more difficult aspects of caring for someone with dementia. Please do not let it deter you from caring for your loved one and enjoying public spaces and venues together. Doing so will make both your lives richer.

CHAPTER 5

Palliative Care and Hospice

Palliative care is available for patients with dementia. While I did not avail myself of these services, I strongly urge you to consider palliative care sooner rather than later. It is a collaborative medical specialty that can provide many services. Unlike with hospice care, you may seek additional treatment while receiving palliative care. My husband was already in late-stage dementia before I came to understand the value of palliative care.

While palliative care can be available to patients with dementia at any stage, hospice care is available only in the latest stages of the disease, and the criteria for acceptance into hospice care can be very stringent. All of the following criteria must be met before a person with dementia is eligible for hospice care: first, they must not be able to walk without assistance; second, they must need assistance in order to dress themselves; third, they must be unable to bathe themselves; fourth, they must be incontinent of both bowel and bladder;

and finally, they must not be able to speak more than a few words in response to questions.

Hospice care is valuable not just for the patient but also for the family. Hospice care nurses are knowledgeable about all aspects of death and dying, and they share this knowledge with the family so that they are able to understand how their loved one's body is shutting down in the dying process. They are there for the family after death as well, and they will help guide you through the grieving process.

Some of the early signs that a patient with dementia is dying include frequent refusal of food and water. Weight loss is profound. They begin to turn inward, interacting with those around them less and less. In the end, my dear husband did not acknowledge my presence at all. On one occasion while I waited with him for his lunch to arrive, he responded to me in single words only, and when asked if he wanted a bath, he skipped lunch altogether, leaving me without a word. Within days of this event, he fell, injuring his shoulder. For the first time, he suffered pain. He was hospice eligible. Within a week, he was gone.

CHAPTER 6

Grief

Grief is a well-defined process.

1. Denial: "This is not happening."
2. Anger: "How dare this happen to me?"
3. Bargaining: "I will give up anything to stop this from happening."
4. Depression: "What is there to live for? Why am I alive?"
5. Acceptance: "This has happened, I must move on, to the best of my ability."

The stages of grief can be very protracted for caregivers of people with dementia. The grieving process is described as "the long goodbye." In my case, going through the stages of grief took eleven years. As a physician, I knew very well what the course of the disease would be, but I still believed we could beat it. When I realized that we could not, anger set in. I was angry at everyone except my dear husband. He was trying his best every single day. Those with whom I was angry had no clue what was going on. They did not even know of the diagnosis. In a way, I was already isolating myself. I knew instinctively that when I revealed the diagnosis, my friends would scatter. They did; I found myself alone.

Yes, I became depressed. I realized that my attitude was very negative and that no matter how hard someone tried to help me, I felt only resentment. I felt they were not doing enough. These are signs of depression. I asked my physician to prescribe an antidepressant medication. This helped a lot. I was no longer so overwhelmed, and I began to appreciate those who were trying to help. I strongly suggest that you consider using antidepressants; you will likely see the benefit.

Unlike those who lose a loved one suddenly or in a short period of time, you will go through the grieving process twice. You will be losing your loved one a brain cell at a time, so your grief will begin as you watch it happen. You will grieve again when they are gone. Many will come alongside you for the funeral. Then they will be gone. I found myself in a kind of shock. Several months passed, and I have no memory of that time. I was existing, not living. Then one day it was over, and I was able to return to writing my first book, *How to Navigate the Minefield That Is Dementia with Your Loved One*. So once again there was purpose.

I also realized that the solitude was not good for me. I needed to put myself in a situation where I could be around other people. I spent time exploring my options. I soon realized that staying in our home was not the best idea. I needed to move forward.

As winter approached, I knew that I would be even more isolated in this harsh Midwestern season. My goddaughter lived in San Diego, and she urged me to visit this delightful city.

I decided to go for the winter. I packed up my poodle, my laptop, and some clothes, and off we went in early November. By mid-January, I knew that I wanted to live in San Diego. I called the real estate agent, and the house was sold on February 1. My poodle and I drove back to St. Louis to sign the papers and contract with the movers. By March 1 we were back to our new home in San Diego.

I have been told how brave I was to make this kind of move at seventy-five. Moving forward is not really hard; what is hard for most people is embracing change. In fact, the world and our lives are always changing. Living requires embracing change. A move such as the one I made is certainly not for everyone. You need to determine for yourself where you want to be when the next change comes along, because it will come.

CHAPTER 7

News from the Front Lines of Research

In mid-2022, the lid blew off a significant portion of Alzheimer's disease research. Much of the millions, if not billions, of dollars spent in the last decade or more have been based on the results of a 2006 study of rats in which amyloid beta appeared to cause dementia. Beginning in 2021 a closer look at these research papers indicated that many of the images in the work had been tampered with. To be fair, the research in question is not the only research that points to amyloid beta. Many scientists are still of the opinion that amyloid beta is the real culprit.

Much of the work to find a cure has been directed at removing the "cause," amyloid beta. Many drugs were tested and were successful at removing amyloid beta from the brains of patients with Alzheimer's disease, but they did little or nothing to alter the course of the disease. Most were associated with severe side effects, the most notable of which was bleeding in the brain. Some scientists believe that testing drugs on patients decades before symptoms develop may be the answer.

Perhaps the best-known culmination of this research path is the FDA approval of Aduhelm in 2021. In the scientific community, this was met with a firestorm of controversy. The cost of treatment with this drug is estimated to be $56,000 per patient per year, and it may well be higher. Many physicians question the safety and effectiveness of the drug. Many well-known health care systems are refusing to prescribe the drug to their patients.

Scientists and drug manufacturers have been sold on amyloid beta as the root cause long enough that many drugs similar to Aduhelm are still in the drug pipeline worldwide. A Swiss drug maker announced in June 2022 that its amyloid beta blocker failed to prevent dementia in asymptomatic but at-risk patients who received the drug for five to eight years.

Despite this, I still have great hope for the future. I believe every day brings us closer to the cure. There are other avenues of research that I believe are more promising, and I will mention several of these in the next few pages.

Money is often not a problem in dementia research. Money is usually available. The factor often missing is research subjects. I urge people with dementia to seriously consider volunteering for studies searching for a cure. Dementia is a fatal disease at the moment, but you could be the first to be cured as a study volunteer. At any rate, you will at least contribute to the knowledge leading to a cure. As the guardian of your loved one, you may include them in relevant studies.

The need for participants in research studies is especially true of racial minorities, since they are underrepresented in most research studies but have a higher incidence of dementia than Caucasians. We need cures that will work for all.

Another abnormal protein, tau, is also found in the brains of people with Alzheimer's disease. Tau is found inside the brain cells. Many scientists have long believed that tau is the root cause of dementia. Several studies published in late 2021 and 2022 suggest that this may well be the case. It should be noted that ALZ-801 administered orally has been shown to significantly reduce abnormal tau protein in treated patients. More recently this drug has been through phase-two trials that show that it can help patients with early dementia and may even be able to prevent it. Patients are seeing brain matter preservation and positive memory effects. Phase-three trials are underway and will take at least a year and half. The drug now has a name: valiltramiprosate. Watch for it; this one really looks good.

A late 2021 study looked at atomoxetine, a drug already in use to treat attention deficit hyperactivity disorder (ADHD). Early results suggest that treatment with this drug does reduce levels of the tau protein and also show increased activity in parts of the brain associated with memory. Side effects were minor. More data is needed to determine whether the drug improves symptoms in patients with dementia.

The fact that this drug is already approved by the FDA for the treatment of ADHD means that if it does improve dementia symptoms, it will be available for patients soon after it is proven effective. Be on the lookout for this drug.

The brain has its own immune system called microglia. Changes in these cells are known to be associated with Alzheimer's disease and dementia. In August 2022, researchers at UC San Francisco reported making strides with gene therapy to return these cells to normal. Much more work must be done before this technique reaches clinical practice, but it is certainly plausible that the cure could be gene therapy.

Human trials have begun on the drug BMS-984923. This one is aimed at improving communication between brain cells, which is lost in patients with dementia. It does seem to have a positive effect on mice. We shall see.

Alzheimer's disease has been called type 3 diabetes because there is an element of insulin resistance involved. New drugs are being developed to prevent this insulin resistance. In addition, drugs such as sulfonylureas already approved for the treatment of type 2 diabetes are being looked at for Alzheimer's disease treatment.

Enormous strides are being made in the search for a cure. These include designer antibodies to inhibit abnormal protein binding, stem cell regenerative treatments (stem cells can now be derived from tissue other than aborted fetuses), DNA manipulation to turn genes on and off, and many others. It will take some time, but I truly believe we are close to finding a cure.

CHAPTER 8

Pearls of Wisdom

Caring for a loved one who has dementia can certainly be difficult, but it can also be associated with moments of great joy. I have shared with you the secrets to help you find that joy.

1. Take Care of Yourself. Make any necessary changes in your life to help yourself prevent dementia. Make those same changes for your loved one. The two of you can share in this journey of self-care.

2. Remember That Dementia Is Aging in Reverse. I believe that this is the most important fact that will help you understand the disease progression. This understanding will help guide your actions and reactions in a way similar to how you would deal with a child. Dealing with a child is sometimes challenging but always joyful. Unlike with a child, however, teaching moments are not useful for either you or your loved one. People with dementia cannot learn, only forget.

3. Quality of Life Is More Important Than Quantity of Life. A basic human need is to be able to accomplish something. In the case of someone with dementia, this may be small indeed but not less important. Just like the child, the person with dementia wants to help. Let them fulfill this basic human need. Let them be of service to you. It will pay dividends for both of you. Another basic human need is risk-taking. Risk-taking in the young is quite obvious but less so in adults with dementia. For people with dementia, it is risky to get up; they might fall. It is risky to go outside; they might get lost. Having quality of life involves some risk. You both need a quality life. Do things together: go to the movies, the ball game, the lecture, and more. If your loved one does something unexpected and inappropriate, don't be embarrassed. Simply notify those around you that your loved one has dementia and a brain age of two. Both of you will find the JOY.

4. Mind, Body, and Spirit Are One. When the mind is failing, build up the body and the spirit. Exercise is so important for both of you. Go for long walks in nature if possible, and if not possible, use a treadmill or home gym or take a tai chi class together. Music is a great way to reach the spirit. Any genre will do. All is uplifting. Go to the symphony or musical theater.

5. Plan Ahead. Step number one is to consult an elder care attorney. You will need a variety of legal documents to protect both of you and your family. Nearly everyone needs help with long-term care. Medicare does not cover this. Between forty-five and sixty-five percent of long-term care is covered by state-administered Medicaid plans. The elder care attorney can help you get this much-needed care without creating financial hardship. Research the long-term care facilities near you. Make sure you fully understand their policies and procedures so you will not be caught unaware. The good facilities will have waiting lists. Get on these lists before you need placement. You can always go to the bottom of the list if you are not ready at the time you are called.

6. Nothing You Do or Do Not Do Will Change the Course of Dementia. Do the best that you can. Never look back with regrets. "If only I had done this or that" does not apply.

7. You Will Go through the Five Stages of Grief Twice. The first time is while you lose your loved one, a brain cell at a time. The second time is after they are gone.

8. Move On. When your loved one's journey with dementia is done, move on with your life. Your loved one would want this for you. Honor their wishes.

9. There Is Hope; the Cure Is Near. Researchers are making great strides toward a meaningful treatment of dementia.

www.ingramcontent.com/pod-product-compliance
Lightning Source LLC
LaVergne TN
LVHW012054070526
838201LV00083B/4681